AN ANTHOLOGY OF
CONTEMPORARY ROMANIAN
POETRY

with best wishes

Brenda Walker

24.8.84.

For Margareta Dobrescu

AN ANTHOLOGY OF CONTEMPORARY ROMANIAN POETRY

TRANSLATED

BY

ANDREA DELETANT
and
BRENDA WALKER

FOREST BOOKS
LONDON * 1984 * BOSTON

Published by FOREST BOOKS
20 Forest View, Chingford, London E4 7AY, U.K.
61 Lincoln Road, Wayland, MA. 01778, U.S.A.

First published 1984

Typeset in Great Britain by Cover to Cover, Cambridge
Printed in Great Britain by A. Wheaton & Co. Ltd., Exeter

Jacket design © Ann Evans
Translations © Andrea Deletant, Brenda Walker

British Library Cataloguing in Publication Data
1. Romanian poetry – Translations into English.
2. English poetry – Translations from Romanian.
I. Deletant, Andrea   II. Walker, Brenda
859'.134'08   PC871.E3
ISBN 0-950948-74-8

Library of Congress Catalog Card Number 84-81308

Cover photograph:
Sculpture
PRAYER
Constantin Brâncuşi 1876–1957
1907/bronze/Art Museum of the Socialist Republic of Romania. Bucharest.

Contents

Preface

Romanian is a Romance language that developed almost two thousand years ago from Latin, then spoken in the region of the lower Danube, and the Romanians today are the only East European people to speak such a language. Grammatically, Romanian differs from the other Romance languages (French, Portuguese, Italian, and Spanish) by preserving a case system and by suffixing the definite article. Although its vocabulary is essentially of Latin origin, Romanian has also been influenced at various times by Slavonic, Greek and Turkish. The spoken rhythms, however, remain notably iambic, which facilitates a close translation of Romanian poetry into English.

In his recent anthology of Romanian Poetry (Editura Eminescu, Bucharest, 1982) Dan Duțescu points out that:

"The so-called outward trimmings of poetry – rhythms, rhyme, alliteration, assonance, as well as onomatopoeia – are not, when we have to do with true poetry, mere additions, mere tags, trinkets and trimmings and trappings and tinkling bells, but the substance and grain of poetic matter itself."

In this anthology, we have attempted to retain the substance and grain within each poet's individual style.

While poets in Romania do not always admit to being influenced by each other, they do admit to the influence of their "Last Romantic"[1], Mihail Eminescu (1850–1889) whose importance for Romanian literature they liken to that of Shakespeare and Chaucer in English literature. Eminescu, with themes drawn from the past, from Romanian folk literature and from his own experience, and expressed in a language enriched by the use of archaisms and the adoption of neologisms, raised Romanian verse to new heights.

At the turn of the century, some Romanian poets experimented with the techniques of symbolism. The verse of George Bacovia (1881–1957) is distinguished by its musicality, its use of mood colours and a repetition of key words, which highlights the monotony and pessimism of his interior contemplation.[2] His contemporaries Tudor Arghezi, Ion Barbu, Lucian Blaga and Vasile Voiculescu gave Romanian poetry its golden age. Arghezi's prosodic innovation and rugged metaphor introduced a new dimension, but it is Blaga, with his philosophic verse, often expressed in symbols and myths, to whom many contemporary poets acknowledge a debt.

The postwar Stalinist era was a period of literary sterility. A number of poets, such as Nina Cassian, commenced writing at this time, but others, such as Ştefan Augustin Doinaş, were unable to publish until the mid-sixties. Those who had established themselves before the war ceased to be acknowledged officially.

However, the release in 1964 of thousands of political prisoners signalled the relaxation of the Romanian régime's rigidity and this was rapidly reflected in the country's cultural life. Barbu, Blaga and Voiculescu were posthumously rehabilitated. Censorship became less strict allowing a sudden blossoming of new literature in which a group of young poets emerged. Among them were Ioan Alexandru, Ana Blandiana, Constanţa Buzea, Nichita Stănescu (who died at the age of fifty in December 1983) and Marian Sorescu. Up to the present time, this group of poets has remained the most widely read and respected by public and critics alike. Their styles are very different, yet each of the poets in his or her own way reflects the "anguish of being".

Marin Sorescu's humorous, yet cogent irony, and anecdotal characters set his style apart from the more ornate, ambiguous or intellectual poetry of many of his contemporaries. His style is characterised by an unexpected and ironic substitution for the predicted conclusion of a colloquial phrase.

Ana Blandiana shares Ioan Alexandru's stark dramatic vision and spiritual qualities, but she also expresses an affinity with nature, where hair can "take root", or backs grow together like "two branches". Her sensitivity for the human condition is reflected not only in "The Couple" and "Torquato Tasso", but also in her latest poems "Courage", "Outburst" and "Suspicion".

Ioan Alexandru's spirituality is rural, portraying ancient rituals, the destiny of "his village" being linked to that of the cosmos. His dramatic skill and ear for dialogue is well exemplified in such ironic portrayals as "The End of the War".

A vein of anxiety permeates Nina Cassian's poetry. There is a strong presence of a destructive force, often felt first in nature, as in her poem "Dank Steps". However, her more sententious poems encapsulate moments of everyday experience common to all.

Constanţa Buzea's melodious verse poignantly reflects human relationships and the bitter taste left by loneliness.

It is said of Ştefan Augustin Doinaş that he puts form before emotion, portraying a "post romantic classicism". Our selection reflects his intellectual rigour and an equilibrium between expression and lyricism.

In many of the later poems of Nichita Stănescu there is an obsession with death. His self-irony and surrealistic imagery often related to animism offer a vision of a single life in which all take part.

Since the early 1970s there has been a wealth of new poetry, from which we have selected six poems by Ion Stoica. His lyricism owes a debt to Blaga, yet he has an originality which produces a fluidity of movement through time and space, fusing thought with feeling.

Our aim in this anthology is to introduce the reader to the work of several of the most significant contemporary Romanian poets. In a future volume we hope to provide a wider selection of 20th century Romanian verse. Most of the poems here, as far as we are aware, have not been previously translated into English.

A special word of thanks is owed to all those who have encouraged us in this undertaking.

Andrea Deletant
Brenda Walker

[1] *The Last Romantic*, Roy MacGregor-Hastie, University of Iowa Press, 1972.
[2] *Plumb/Lead*, George Bacovia, Translated by Peter Jay, Foreword by Marian Popa, Minerva Publishing House, Bucharest, 1980.

Acknowledgments

Poems in this anthology have been taken from the following volumes:

Ioan Alexandru
Poeme 1970 (Editura Eminescu, Bucureşti)

Ana Blandiana
Cincizeci De Poeme 1970 (Editura Eminescu, Bucureşti)
Octombrie, Noiembrie, Decembrie 1972
(Editura Cartea Românească, Bucureşti)
Somnul Din Somn 1977 (Editura Cartea Românească, Bucureşti)
Ora De Nisip 1983 (Editura Eminescu, Bucureşti)

Constanţa Buzea
Poeme 1977 (Editura Albatros, Bucureşti)

Nina Cassian
De Indurare 1981 (Editura Eminescu, Bucureşti)

Ştefan Aug. Doinaş
Alfabet Poetic 1978 (Editura Minerva, Bucureşti)

Marin Sorescu
Poeme 1965 (Editura Pentru Literatura, Bucureşti)
Moartea Ceasului 1966 (Editura Tineretului, Bucureşti)
Tuşiţi 1970 (Editura Eminescu, Bucureşti)
Fîntîni In Mare 1982 (Editura Eminescu, Bucureşti)

Nichita Stănescu
Epica Magna 1978 (Editura Junimea, Iaşi)

Ion Stoica
Porţile Clipei 1982 (Editura Albatros, Bucureşti)

Ioan Alexandru
(b. 1941)

IMAGE

I see my father holding a huge loaf in his arms
by the light of the lamp.
For the little sister he cuts a little slice,
for the larger boy, he cuts a larger slice,
for the biggest brother, the biggest slice,
and Mama's left to cut her own in her corner
near the hearth where night's already fallen,

and then time appears, a powerful whirlwind,
no one can stand aside.
In the middle of the house on the face of that earth,
three paths appear chiselled in stone,
different, full of smoke and sweat falls —
and rusted chill.

The crumbling roof breaks
and damp leaves fall in the corner of the lane
and one autumn morning
a boy rises to the sky
and all the village is lit by his image
as by a new planet.
And graves in the earth widen
where greying ages withdraw
for eternity of the snows.

THE END OF THE WAR

When I come into the world war were endin',
Last orders were shot. On field
Last canons were hung by their shadows.
In our house presents were shared.

'First to you, John,' said the War to father, from the corner of the
                                                        table,
'Because you have served me faithfully,
I hand you this wooden leg.
Wear it in memory of me, and good health to you.
It's sturdy from the trunk of an old oak;
When you die the woods will rock you
Like a brother in the summits of their eyes.
Your right hand, because it has no book learning anyway,
I wrenched from your elbow and have given it to the earth
To teach it to write.

'For you, Maria,' said the War to mother –
'Because you watered my horses with your tears
And left two sons on the battlefield
To polish my boots, and brought up
Two maidens with whom I've spent my nights,
Look, I'll give you this beautiful bunch of white hair
To adorn your temples
And this even bigger bunch of wakeful nights,
As well as this empty house without a roof.

To you, George, son of Peter from over the hill, –
For the two hazel eyes, you say you had,
Look, I give you possession of all the boundaries of darkness,
So you can harvest them, you and your wife
Forever.

For the village, I leave only forty orphans
Under six months, ten empty houses and the others in ruins,
Also, the sky towards sunset, half burned.
The tower without bells; eight women in the cemetery
Hung with heads to the ground, and twenty horses dead from the
                                                neighbour's farm.

2

For you, just born, because anyway we don't know each other very
                                                well,
I leave the cows udder dry,
The plum trees burned alive in the garden,
The eye of the well, dead,
And may the sky feed you on its stars.
And I baptize you in the name of the Lord.

APPARITION

In rain crammed on the sea,
in a broken hut
we prepared for the journey to earth.
Long lightning all the night,
waters groaned in grey whirlpools,
and putrid planks creaked underfoot.
Alone and without sleep,
when the crucified one on the cross, alive, bleeding,
appeared over us. We huddled in awe,
what were we hoping? When his arms were heard blasting
in our breast. Were we burning? Were we sleeping?
Or had we died long ago?
The cross and pale beard disappeared in the deep
pulled by heavenly ropes towards immortal horizons.

AS IN PARADISE

Our cemetery is common land
surrounded by a stone fence,
so as not to be caught by earth
left alive in liberty.

The wooden crosses, after a few years
lean on one side and then also die
forever, and strange men come
on wild mares and steal them
for their fires.

The plot of the grave is wiped away —
wiry grass clutters everywhere
like hair on heads of the young on winter nights;
when the cemetery is full to the brim from one end
to the other, everything starts again from the beginning;
the grave of my grandfather is on the grave of my great
                                        grandfather,
my father over my grandfather,
and likewise the old mayor
over the age-old mayor— the old priest
over the age-old priest,
the old village over the ancient village.

At the edges grow plum and apple trees
And scented flowers can be seen,
their vapour penetrates into things
far away.
Those who come passing by here
with watches buried in their left wrist
and shoulders full of old age
marvel as in paradise.

JOB

After Job lost his last son
He began to convince himself that from now on death
Was his only companion. So near he drew to it
And gradually confessed to it, that for Job another life began.
The one without risk, without advice, without hope,
Without the simplest longing, without repentance,
Without blemish. Faith was no longer a fortress
To be conquered by devotion.
He lost all sense of action, all sense of temptation,
For some time then the flesh on his body had left him.
His eyes turned in upon himself, hands motionless. –
Job was passing into the other world without any regret,
Without any knowledge,
Just as were born and died the dead
Before the birth of God.

MY SISTER

None of you who are my age
can know my elder sister,
nor do I know her other than from sleep
and oblivion.
In hazy weather in the long lost autumn,
she died before I was born
and so hurried my coming
to that empty place left in the world.
That's why I'm also taller,
grown in her shade,
and have reached more quickly the age of doubt.

I'm preparing for autumn in full spring
and in summer I hear the frost of winter in my bones,
I carry through the world my sister's void,
When I die, I'll have been dead a long time.

Ana Blandiana
(b. 1942)

A VILLAGE

More of a smell
Than image or sound,
The smell of smoke in the evening,
Especially when the herds return, dizzy
From too much milk flowered in the fields;
Smell of milk making a froth,
Pulled erotically from the udder, as if
Coupling in its blue flesh
The green soul of wild grass
With the gentle, moving
Breath of smoke;
The smell of wet straw
And heaps of berries,
Smell of wheat pyramids rising to the sky,
While the air of evening seeps back into itself
And clouds unfold
Into brief stories and vanish;
The smell of self,
Of hair long in the sun,
Of skin for herbs dreaming,
Of sleep and of word –
A village built on air
From endless seeming,
Loved with one's breath
And rocked by the wind!

A MEETING

Don't be afraid.
Everything will be so easy
That you won't even understand
Until much later.
You will wait at the beginning
And only when
You begin to believe
That I don't love you anymore
Will it be hard for you,
But then I will make
A blade of grass grow
In our corner of the garden,
To reach out
And whisper:
Don't be afraid,
She's fine
And waiting for you
Near these roots of mine.

TORQUATO TASSO[1]

He came from the darkness towards me, the poet,
The poet who failed because of fear.
He was very handsome. As on an X-ray
You could see the poetry on his body,
Poetry unwritten through fear.
"I am mad" – he said. A fact I knew
From the foreword to his books.
But like a password he carried his madness
To enter here, as if he would say
"I redeem myself thus
For in my poems there's lack of truth.
The price is immense. I approach you. Receive me!"
But I answered: Go away from here!

"I wrote at the flames of the Inquisition" – he told me –
"Feeling on my body
The hair shirt singeing.
My room had monks' eyes for windows
And their ears stuck to each other, for doors,
And mice coming out of their holes were monks,
And at night huge birds wore habits to sing to me.
You must understand . . ." And with a finger he pointed
Showing in my body the poetry there,
The unwritten poetry . . .
But I shouted: Go away from here!

---

[1] Italian poet (1544–1595) who died on the brink of insanity.

WEARINESS

What unassuming dead we have!
Through volcanoes they've never erupted,
Even with walls built upon them
They do not stir.
With gestures carved by others
They let themselves be held in statues,
They let flags be harnessed to them
On unknown roads,
They let themselves be ploughed and dutifully rot
To feed the earth
What unassuming dead we have
And wearied.

DO YOU REMEMBER THE BEACH?

Covered with painful fragments
Do you remember the beach
On which
We couldn't walk barefoot,
The way
You were looking at the sea
And saying you were listening to me?
Do you remember
The frantic seagulls
Wheeling in the ringing
Of unseen church bells
Whose patrons were fishes,
And how
You distanced yourself running
Towards the sea
Calling to me
That you needed distance
To look at me?
The snow
Was dying
Stirred with the birds
In the water,
With an almost happy despair
I was watching
The prints of your steps on the sea
And the sea
Was closing like an eyelid
Over the eye in which I waited.

FALLING ASLEEP

I fall asleep, you fall asleep,
The way we stay with eyes closed
Stretched next to each other
We seem two youths equally dead.
Listen how sleepily rustles the sun
Through the dried grasses,
The sky is soft and leaves on the fingers
A sort of pollen.
Over our faces move
The shadows of flocks of birds,
The smell of grapes seeps into us.
Fall asleep,
Don't be afraid,
Our neighbouring hair strands
Spread on the grass
Have begun to take root,
Soon the leaves will cover us
In the golden snow.
We've never looked more alike,
Your wings have sunk into the earth
And cannot be seen any more.

KEEP YOUR EYES CLOSED

Keep your eyes closed,
Keep your eyes closed,
It's only given to us once,
I ask you nothing
The snow settles down.
It's buried the cemetery and the village
It's walling up the church,
Tops of poplars can still be seen above
Like grass growing.
The snow settles and leavens
As a field fermenting
Which will soon stop
The time from above falling.
Keep your eyes closed
It's only given to us once
And only once must we give.
I ask you nothing, only
Wait for the last time-flake to set
And void becomes the sky,
And in silence, only then
Unfold your left arm from the nails
And send the snow-glass gently turning.

ASLEEP

Asleep
I happen to cry out,
Only when asleep,
And frightened by my own daring
I wake,
In the well disciplined silence of night,
And try to hear
Cries from neighbours' sleep.
But the neighbours are wise
Crying out only when they're sure
That they dream they're asleep.
In the sleep within sleep
Where no one can hear,
They give way to cries.
What free uproar
Must be there,
In the sleep within sleep.

A COUPLE

Some only see you,
Others see only me,
We superimpose so perfectly
That no-one can spot us at the same time
And no-one dares to live on the edge
From where we can both be seen.
You only see the moon,
Only I see the sun,
You yearn for the sun,
I yearn for the moon,
But we stay back to back,
Bones united long ago,
Our blood carries rumours
From one heart to the other.
What are you like?
If I lift my arm
And stretch backwards
I discover your sweet shoulder-blade
And, going upwards, the fingers touch
Your divine lips,
Then suddenly return
To crush my mouth, bleeding.
What are we like?
We have four arms for defence
But only I can hit the enemy here
And only you the enemy there,
We have four legs to run,
But you can only run on your side
And I on mine.
Every step's a life and death struggle.
How equal are we?
Are we to die together or will one of us carry,
For a time
The corpse of the other stuck to our side
Infecting with death, slowly, too slowly,
Or perhaps never to die completely
But carry for an eternity
The sweet burden of the other,
Atrophied forever,

The size of a hunch,
The size of a wart . . .
Oh, only we know the longing
To look into each other's eyes
And so at last understand,
But we stay back to back,
Grown like two branches
And if one should tear away,
Sacrificing all for a single look,
You would only see of the other
The back from which you came
Bleeding, shivering,
Tearing.

WHEN I'M ALIVE

When I'm alive in my dream
On earth I've died
And when I'm still here
Am I dead inside?

Or is it only a game
With a moon and sun
Who sadistically share me
Ruling as one?

When it's night here
In sleep it's light –
I come back unwilling
From dream and from life.

IT'S SNOWING

It's snowing with malice,
The snow falls with hate
Above waters icy with loathing,
Above orchards blossomed by evil,
Above embittered birds who suffer,
It snows as if the acquatic dweller
Would feel this life ebbing,
It snows
With human drive, –
Venomously it's snowing.
Who then to surprise?
Only I know
That once a flurry of snow
Was love, at the beginning. –
It's so late
And hideously it's snowing,
And my mind's stopped working
So I wait
For it to be of use
This wolf that's starving.

IN THE MORNING AFTER DEATH

In the morning after death
It will be cold as in the misty dawns of September,
When from the lustful scorching heat of summer
I come round in the white air,
A stranger to the trees, light entangled, woollen,
I will be woken, as in September, early
And, as in September,
Alone enough to hear
The air as it drips towards noontime
On the cheek of wet quinces.
And I will be tired,
And beg to stay asleep,
A little longer,
Lying without motion,
With eyes closed, face to the cushion,
While the deafening silence
Will awake me more and more,
To begin,
Like a morning in autumn,
Eternal daytime.

ONLY WITH ME

Only with me
And so reconciled
Under the last sun,
Almost faded in the orchard
So that I can hear
The colours in the leaves flowing
And the gentle rustling
Of the soft clouds.
Only with me.
Such a good silence.
Nothing to say.

SO COLD

So cold that saliva freezes
On dogs' teeth
While they howl to the moon
Going mad with fear.
So cold my lips tear
With terror when I shout
And with the blood, still warm,
I lick it like a beast.

A CHURCH FULL OF
BUTTERFLIES

A church full of butterflies,
Icons dusty with pollen,
Drowned in a silence poisoned
By slow movement of wings
Deep and rhythmic;
A church in which
Antennae
Cringe at the tips
Blindly touching the altar,
While the light
The crumbly light tumbles
Above the ambiguous rustle
Of cloaks of saints
And wings . . .
I sit in the pew rigid
Terrified their flight
May touch me,
Understanding why I know everything –
I made the clumsy drawing
On the wings
In my childhood,
When I first learned to write,
The church much later,
Forgetting,
On the same paper . . .

PIETA

The clear pain, the death has brought me back,
Submitted to your arms, almost a child.
You don't know whether to be thankful
Or cry
For such happiness,
Mother.
My body, stripped of the mystery
Is yours alone.
Sweet your tears drip onto my shoulder
And gather obediently near the blade.
How good it is!
The pilgrimages and words never to be understood,
The disciples, of whom you're proud, of whom you are afraid,
The Father, the assumed, the unspoken, watching,
All is behind.
Calmed by the understood suffering
You hold me in your arms
And stealthily
You rock me, gently,
Rock me, Mama.
Three days only, I'm allowed to rest
In death and on your lap.
Then the resurrection will come
And again you are not meant to understand.
Three days only,
But until then
I feel so good
On your lap, descended from the cross,
If I wasn't afraid you'd find it terrifying,
Gently I'd turn my mouth
To your breast, suckling.

SO SIMPLE

Oh, if only I were a candle,
To waste gradually
From one end to the other,
Simply, as in sums
Of children . . .
My mind first – what happiness! –
Would disappear.
People would say
"How mindless is this girl!"
I'd remember nothing
Nor attempt to understand.
My heart would then melt
And I'd love no more,
Hate no more,
No suffering would reach me,
And people would say
"How heartless is this girl!"
And again, again
And then not one wish more
No passion,
And my blood, carrier of ships
Would scatter,
To leave only
Shrivelled knees,
Shaking with dignity or kneeling.
No one would even speak.
In the last silence,
The wax pool
Especially punished, cooled
For the horrific shadows which
Its light brought into the world.

WINGS

Churches don't have roofs,
But wings shivering on bodies
Of wooden tiles,
Soon the time will come
For them to open
And rise
Slowly, as if reluctantly,
Carrying their beings
Of gold and smoke
Into the air higher and higher,
Flying with great roaring, like
A flock of heavy birds
Towards sunset,
While the mountains, in panic,
Mixed with sea
Rushing towards them
Would unfurl –
For the world a beautiful ending
Under the life blue sky
Swarming with great churches
Living.

SUSPICION

Does the flower have liberty
When everything's fixed,
The precise date
When it blooms and dies,
The smell
It's supposed to emit
And the colour which sets it alight?
It says yes.
And the petals say yes, each in turn,
And the stamins, and pollen grains,
And the leaves and the thin, fragile
Stems. Yes.
But what then is liberty? I ask
A little embarrassed by suspicion of the reply
What a question! amazed,
The angel blinked his petals.

SOOT

What do you think about when you see
An archangel covered in soot?
Of the pollution of the stratosphere, of course.
And what else?
Of the habit of angels
To find their way into everything.
And what else?
Of the chimney in spring beginning
To smoke and get clogged-up.
And what else?
Oh, if I think hard,
An archangel covered in soot
Could also be an archangel who
Set himself on fire
Forgetting he couldn't burn.

OUTBURST

At each outburst
A god unfolds
Blowing large folds
Of his cloak across the sky.
There are so many kinds of gods
On earth
That we'll never be able
To laugh or cry enough
To entice them from where they hide.
Whether laughter or tears,
It doesn't really matter:
Important is the outburst.

COURAGE

I'm looking at my hands:
Little fronds where
Eyelids of leaves
Never blink;
Tips of wings where
Feathers haven't dared
To increase;
And at the ends,
Not even claws have been able
To spring up as
Gentle buds of a beast.
I look at my hands
As I would at letters
Which haven't the courage
To make themselves.
Into a word.

Constanţa Buzea
(b. 1942)

THERE WHERE I THINK YOU ARE

There where I think you are,
Not even trains pass,
The forests of frosty firs
Appear there like glass.

Further and further away you feel,
Always added to the rest, and still.
I cannot go forward
Unless I lose myself as well.

And all time breathes white,
White are roads in the snow,
I wouldn't even recognise you now
Without the pair of us, without a halo.

I feel pity when remembering,
Yet can't bring myself to forget
How much illusion is in destiny,
How many mistakes can be met.

As if from under a snowed up shawl
With cold fingers I gather
Our soul, still sincere,
With its movement towards silver.

The way it snows, it may not stop,
And the firs would be encircled there,
Amongst barbarian meteorites,
There where I think you are.

Every year I wait
For the snow, so that I can see you,
See if you look, if you listen,
If you understand a little more now.

31

THE NAIVE REWARDING OF ONE WHO LIES

The same old journeys and the same old aims,
The same old pigeons on a bowl of lentils,
The naive rewarding of the one who lies.

I'm longing for rest and for holy things,
For full and bitter tears,
For humility and for prayers
Towards the sadness of mothers' graves.

Because few words I'm saddled with,
They're hung round my neck, and my mind demands
An eye for an eye, and a tooth for a tooth.

SPEAK WELL OF ME

Speak well of me, to those who trespass against me.
Into my own soul I fall as in a pit
Whenever I stay lying down in grass near water
Like a death it's afraid of me.

In my dream grazes a white herd,
And autumn appears the same everywhere.
I entrust you with this empty page
So earth will not know how I fared.

Whenever longing is longer than death,
I see before me rings of danger,
My inside betrays me, we cannot be alone,

As far as I can see, a wall of eyes.
It is made insatiable, wildly beautiful
The scene that comes towards home.

THE END OF THE WORLD

Don't let memory keep
All the words,
Our hurtful words,
Beautiful and cold.

Chosen and calmly spoken,
You hardly understand them,
Our hurtful words,
When they leave, you bury them.

There is silver and shadows of kings
At the end of the world,
Our hurtful words,
Beautiful and cold.

THE SIN OF PRIDE

The trees shake great birds,
And the vineyards Divine nectar.
The way to me is far,
The way to death is nearer.

I get up every autumn,
It seems a path I can't remember.
The way to me is far,
The way to death is nearer.

These words for harvesting
I feel as desires, yet I know I'm to suffer,
All my love came true
And proved so right for its future.

Why aren't I, as it would appear,
In decline, unhappier!
The way to me is far,
The way to death is nearer.

LOCKED IN THE
ADULT WORLD

Stay a child, yet think
While locked in the adult world.
Stay a child, shyly passing
And listening to words.

If for everyone the wind is blowing,
For you it has a special meaning,
A feeling of immortality.

Be pure, hiding
From others who are sinning,
Be sorry for the clouds,
And for them changing,
For which they're not guilty.

Nina Cassian
(b. 1924)

THAT'S ABOUT IT

More and more often,
more and more painfully,
I remember something else:
how a child once pulled faces at me,
how all the addresses where I lived
had names of plants,
the smell of my drawing book
and, after that,
the atmosphere of a kiss which embraced me,
kisses to suffocation I walked and breathed,
and, after that, sacks with the dead
which I carried on my back
and still carry
—well, yes, that's about it,
that would be about it
this is what you'd call my life,
the one in the skin of the sea,
in the garment of the grass,
in the curse of not speaking,
in the labour of not creating.

LIKE ANA

Once I entered with you
into a house of love
and left it fleeing
from misunderstanding,
hating the long street
and the sky with stars.
Then fell the first stone
on my heart.
Now the building is completed.
No more breathing from anyone inside.

DANK STEPS

Spring – a girl on crutches
with cheeks sharp and grey
as an icicle of dirty water
hits dogs and trees
with her crutches
and curses like an old crone.
Windows have wrinkles
and there's heavy thunder.
Spring – a girl
with hair of mud
shapes in mud
human forms
with her crutches.

MORNING EXERCISES

I wake up and say: I'm through.
It's my first thought at dawn.
What a nice way to start the day
with such a murderous thought.

God, take pity on me
– is the second thought, and then
I get out of bed
and live as if
nothing had been said.

WITHOUT GUILT

You don't have to be guilty
to suffer punishment.
Look what happened to the flower!
It had just appeared, pink among leaves,
and the big animal came
and blew an insult all over it.

DOWNHILL

How minute we are.
How hurried we are.
How coarsely we speak.
Only the spider
stayed all night in the same place
on the side of the bath.
– Good morning, eight-legged patient one,
silent witness.

We decline, deteriorate,
when the supreme criteria degenerate.

HORIZON

And yet there must exist
a zone of salvation.
Sad are the countries
who don't have outlets to water,
dull are the people who have no outlet from themselves
toward another outlet, even greater.

OPTICAL ILLUSION

In perfect darkness,
without moon, without lights, without fireflies,
without there, without here,
– a complete peace,
a complete stillness
of black on blackness.

PRESSURES

If the tear
is the egg of the rain bird
if the bird is air full of unease
which itself
is a body over bodies
– how can I write a book
in this communal grave?

IF I HAD DIED IN AN EARTHQUAKE

Who do you want to carry in your arms?
I was a little girl, I was a little boy.
I left childhood
with too large a head,
and entered youth with too small a shoulder.

And when I reached proportions of gold,
a tremor came
a tremor of lead
– why mention it . . .

The poet said: I'm a beautiful memory.

ECHO

Yesterday, I heard again the crashing fall
of the house of the world
and in the silence that followed
I again felt full of awe.

A promiscuous death,
has mingled
life with no life,
something glitters, it's not known
whether it's a needle
or a splinter from my bone.

Ştefan Aug. Doinaş
(b. 1922)

INVOCATION TO NIGHT

Spherical is reality.
At noon dangling,
my eye weeping
darkness for a country.

Only the wide-eyed owl
confirms it, eerily,
his iris ethereally,
keeps it under seal.

Night, possess me!
A thousand things and deeds,
lightning without pity

like stars in a bunch
in my pupil revolving,
smoking it with significance.

LIFE BURNS AWAY AT EITHER END

What is the wisdom of a book compared to the wisdom of an angel?

Hölderlin

Life burns away at either end, with a difference.
    We're only just born, and the divine is in us
        still feeling its way in play, when – look:
           a jungle is now the paradise about us and

only with nails like sickles, only
    with beaks and jaws can salvation be caught
        in flight. Middle-age is hunting,
           and like beasts is hunted daily.

Then, comes enlightened rest,
    when bones still hold
        the evening sun above the plain,
           and the odour of the pale stubble field.

Yes! But who rides the stallion
    now and writes with the iron of the plough?
        Whose grey footwear is
           dusted with smiles, with strands of hair?

Greying angels among suckling ones,
    the divine surrounds us and we play again
        the first game but with hollow beads,
           our gains deducted from losses.

Is this the way we'll sip wisdom?
    Yet how can we taste it, if we haven't left
        souls in the hilts of our swords
           and our mouths on the mouth of the mad?

Life burns away at either end, with a difference,
    for in the evening, when we put out the children with tales,
        the deed they hear is the fire of innocence,
           but the mouth that tells it is ash.

THE WORDS OF THE POET

As birds rise in the skies leaving an empty straw nest
searching for a king of birds, each beady-eyed,
and then day by day above the world the meeting is delayed
until, sensing the flock their loving king, end their quest

so words start searching for that essential instant
which bathes the pulse in moments of brilliance and perpetuity
words more than ever alien as an unendured austerity
divided by potential speech and ever more obedient

until the white page digests them like clusters settling
in which the dead deed blows coolly from meaning.

THE KISS

Like the leaf which floats to the well
I trouble your soul for a kiss,
and your mouth gulping me, stirs
with waves whose needs you can't tell.

Nor does the fire more strongly shudder
nor does the breeze get you drunk any easier.
The leaves on your shoulder, a crackling shower
which fall from a single song.

Why are you sighing? Which cloud enters you?
On your beauty, like waves above you
comes down, lazily, a shadowy shawl.

Ah! On the lips my leaf to ashes is turning . . .
But, the wild vein, rotting,
scratches its image in the soil.

THE NIGHT

We knew it was coming: the mud in the lakes
was turning pink, only the trill
of fading birds still floated in air,
and smoke was rising with an ever
open palm – to receive it; water
was talking to itself near rocks.

We were still together. Simple space
created only with breath, a step
in which begins the furnace.
I held the first star in my right hand,
but only the hand knew it, the gaze
on two paws – waiting for it to arrive.

It oozed gently: with scarabs,
which were beginning to melt in air,
with your eyes, in which our place
was receiving someone strange, and with grass,
where it was forever night.

SEPTEMBER

Silver knife through the gorged heart
of September. Melodiously
travels the sound of brass, and then starts
to go down a semitone, suddenly.
But what light still! . . . Avid wasps
besiege the sweetness: sparkles
on the surface of a sphere which grasps
emptiness of night in its superb wealth.
Will we exist – or not? A mystical feast
of upturned flight is offered us on the wind:
as it is the apple, while setting light
to distance between branch and earth . . .

Marin Sorescu
(b. 1936)

THE TRAVELLER

In memory, the waters I've just come through
Have left a slight sheen under the skin,
I can't run agilely with speed
Unless I have heels covered in blisters,
Unless they feel like a marsh,
Where you sink, imperceptibly.

I can only fall asleep when I crouch
Somewhere on a suitcase near overcrowded
Train doors,
Woken from dozing everytime a passenger gets on
Or gets off.
In these breaks I dream the most beautiful dreams,
All, alas, abruptly interrupted.

Ah, sleep in an average, strange bed
In a third rate hotel!
One falls flat on the greasy divan, damp, slightly cock-eyed,
In the room there's a smell of prison,
The window's barred.
And it'd be stupid to open it because beggers can jump.

About midnight, pain wakes you,
It's in the ribs, made by the springs,
You feel your way and can't find the light.
Where are you? Which town is it?
You think you're still travelling and wait for the guard,
"What's the next station, please?"

Sometimes it's true, you're in the express!
In the sleeper. You decided to treat yourself.
At the window you recognise nothing,
The scenery may just as well

Be Italian, Swiss or even the moon.
Trees change from second to second,
Like guards of honour
At a hasty funeral,
Or like telegrams received in a battle
Where the result's uncertain.
You're the commander, you received them, opened them,
The subalterns are watching your mouth waiting for orders,
But the telegrams are ciphered
And you've forgotten the cipher of the leaves.

I only feel well when
Half-asleep, uncomfortable,
Standing on one foot on a blister
Strap-hanging, hung on a window-sill,
On a servant's stair,
Having to rush urgently God knows where,
Carrying four big suitcases full of useless things,
Relinquishing, because of them, the only thing
Of any importance: the umbrella . (It always rains cats and dogs,
                                    when you're a traveller.)

I only feel well when unwell,
Limping,
Bags under the eyes,
Thrown in the street by my own anxiety . . .

Always pushed about on roads like a kick up the arse,
Eyes bulging, as if I'd seen a miracle.

SYNCHRONIZATION

Everything about us is perfect
On this century's
Cinema screen:
Both in sound and image.

It's just that many times
With appearance on cue,
We start to act and talk sense –
But nothing's heard.
Your words on the screen run ahead
Or get stopped at customs.
At other times you find yourself speaking
Someone else's lines,
Which don't fit your mouth,
They're too big or too small.

Then far worse
Is when your voice begins to be heard
After you've emerged
From the projector's beam
Of sun.

It doesn't matter.
There are a few small defects
Of synchronization.
Perhaps in time we'll be able
To say exactly what we think,
And to speak
Even in our lifetime.

WE TALK ABOUT THE WEATHER

We've finished all topics of conversation,
Now let's talk about the weather,
Any of us can say something
About weather.

I, to start talking,
Will be of the opinion it'll rain,
Because I dreamt of a big cloud
Circling round my brow
Which always rained on me,
Soaking thoughts to the skin.

Someone
To contradict me, insists upon good weather.
For in the following three centuries,
The sky will be so bright
That we'll all see each other,
Without needing fireworks
To do so.

Someone talks to us about a dead leaf,
Which flies before the bare trees
And which none of us can keep –
Tomorrow it'll pass our street,
Let's go on the balcony
And watch it too.

And so we're able to hold a conversation,
We'll contradict each other and speak very loudly,
So that crickets inside us run away hurriedly.

The main thing is that silence never comes between us,
The main thing is to be happy.

THE INVISIBLE ONES

The royal throne is right there in my head,
Or to be more exact, it is my head,
It's all that's left
Of an area as vast as the eye can see.

And over it
How many invasions have spread,
How many trenches must I dig daily
To fill them all with sweat from my brow
– it's fresher, running, and much safer –
To raise turret walls round it,
And in the end defend it sword in hand.

Of course I fight the battle
With the barbarians.
As many as there are grains of sand,
Their numbers darken even the sun,
It's just that they can't be seen,
They're barbarians totally invisible,

That's why the battle's even more terrible
And even more a struggle for life and death,
It's just that I've no blood left to spill
Unless perhaps it's mine again
If I suddenly feel like suicide.

My one wish is that these efforts of mine
Be recorded in the struggle for independence,
And that important historical events
Be given their true significance.

ATAVISM

Looking out of the window has become a nervous tic,
Everyone's looking out of the window.
They read, they wash, they love, die
And from time to time they rush
To look out of the window.

What do you want to see?
Who are you staring at?
Stop thinking about it, who's coming's come,
Who had to go's gone,
What was to pass by, has passed by.
Leave the curtains,
Pull the blinds
And take your blood pressure once again.

Having seen everything, – rain, wars,
Sun, moles, events,
Always repeated exactly the same,
I can't believe mankind seriously wants
To see something else.
However there it is stuck to the window
With hollow eyes.

COMPETITION

One, two, three . . .
The hibernation competition has begun.
Everyone lock yourselves in your lair
And let's see who can hibernate the longest.

You know the competition rules:
No moving,
No dreaming,
No thinking.
Anyone caught thinking
Is out of the game and no longer our concern.

Like a pipe, you can only use
Your paw for sucking
To stimulate you in the deep understanding
Of this event.

I'm lucky to find myself near a bear,
Because when I've had enough of my paw,
I'll give it to him,
And use his,
Which as it happens is within the accepted norm
Of paws.
And although the Pharoah Cheops
Has the advantage of a few milleniums,
I also hope to overtake him
By an outstanding sprint,
Our famous sprint
In the field of hibernation.

*　*　*

Every year
Life salutes us
With 365 shots
Of sun.

It's a great event
Our arrival into the
Inanimate world,
And matter
Gives us our due
Honours.

The trees put on little flags
Of seasons,
In the air, rise oxygen bubbles
And coloured stars.

From the sea cheers are heard,
Waves carry banners.
Everything
Clamours to see us,
What more can I say?
It's a beautiful feast and unrivalled.

And we, moved,
For as long as the light lasts,
Stay standing
As for the national anthem.

TRUTH COMES TO LIGHT

Truth comes to light
Extremely slowly.
Following the movement technique of decomposure and rotting
Oil rises to the surface
But only after it's drowned.

*   *   *

When I want to have a rest
I'm ill.
I take to my bed.
Imagine how ill
I'll be
Dead!

WITH JUST ONE LIFE

Hold with both hands
The tray of each day
And pass in a line
In front of this counter.

There's enough sun
For everyone,
There's enough sky,
There's enough moon.

From the earth comes fragrance
Of luck, happiness, glory
Which tickles your nostrils
Temptingly.

So don't be miserly,
Live as your heart's stirred,
The prices are absurd.

For instance, with just one life
You can get
The most beautiful woman,
And a loaf.

SENTENCE

Each traveller in the tram
Looks identical to the one who sat there before him
On that very seat.

Either the speed's far too great,
Or the world's far too small.

Each has a threadbare neck caused
By the newspaper read behind him.
I'm aware of a newspaper in the neck
Turning and cutting my veins
With its edges.

THE RECKONING

There comes a time
When we have to draw a line under us
A black line
To do the summing up.

The few moments when you were about to be happy,
The few moments when we were nearly beautiful,
The few moments when we were almost a genius.
Occasionally we've met
Mountains, trees, water
(What ever happened to them? Do they still exist?)
Each adds up to a brilliant future –
Which we've lived.

A woman we've loved,
Plus the same woman who didn't love us
Equals zero.

A quarter of a year of studies
Makes several million fodder words
Whose widsom we've gradually eliminated.
And finally, a fate
Plus another fate (Now where does that come from?)
Equals two (Write one, carry one,
Perhaps, who knows, there is a life hereafter).

THE OLD ONES IN THE SHADE

You tire quickly, you forget easily,
You begin to talk alone,
You move your lips . . .
In the mirror you surprise yourself moving your lips.

I know roughly what it's going to be like when I'm old.
Every summer I experience one or two days a week
Of old age.
Wrinkled, dried out like a peach stone in the core
Of a juicy day.

A Ulysses with a mind like a sieve,
Forgetting where he was supposed to return,
Why he wanders on the sea
And whether it's before or after the Trojan wars.
A Ulysses with few chances of kissing the smoke leaving chimneys
Of his homelands.

You hesitate between adjusting your tie
And strangling yourself with it.

40 degrees in the sun! I come into the house
And with a last mental effort remember
What I'm called.
The sultry heat resembles old age.
The same sensations.

The carpet slips from under your feet
You trip over your slippers –
A nail is turning purple,
You seem to have a wobbling tooth.

There's a feeling of unity in summer,
We're all older,
Even the foetus in the womb of the mother.

THE ACTORS

How easy-going – the actors!
With their sleeves rolled up
How cleverly they're able to be us!

I've never seen a more perfect kiss
Than by actors in the third act,
When emotions are beginning
To clear.

Stained with oil
In authentic caps,
Carrying out all kinds of jobs,
They enter and exit on lines
Which roll from their feet like rugs.

So natural is their death on stage
That, compared to this perfection,
The ones in graveyards
Seem to move,
Those who wear forever the make-up of tragedy,
The real dead!

We're stiff and awkward in just one life!
We don't know how to live it properly anyway.
We talk a load of nonsense or keep silent years on end.
And embarrassed and unattractive
We don't know what the hell to do with our hands.

PRAYER

Saints,
Let me join your ranks
At least as an extra.

You're getting old,
Perhaps you feel the pain of age
Painted on your bodies
In so many stages.

Let me carry out
The humblest jobs
In nooks and crannies.

I could for instance,
Eat the light
At the Last Supper,
And blow out your haloes
When the service is over.

And, from time to time,
At half a wall's distance,
Cup my hands to my mouth
And holler, once for the believers
And once for the unbelievers:
Hallelujah! Hallelujah!

SHAKESPEARE

Shakespeare created the world in seven days.

On the first day he made the sky, the mountains and the depths
of the soul.
On the second day he made rivers, seas, oceans
And the other emotions –
And gave them to Hamlet, Julius Caesar, Anthony, Cleopatra
and Ophelia,
To Othello and others,
To be master over them, with their descendants,
For ever and ever.
On the third day he gathered all the people
And taught them to savour:
The taste of happiness, love, despair,
The taste of jealousy, fame and so on,
Until all tasting was finished.
Then some late-comers arrived.
The creator patted their heads with compassion,
Saying the only roles left for them were the
Literary critics
Who could then demolish his work.
The fourth and fifth day he reserved for laughter.
He allowed clowns
To tumble,
He allowed kings, emperors
And other unfortunates to amuse themselves.
On the sixth day he completed the administration:
He set up a tempest,
He taught King Lear
How to wear a straw crown.
As there were a few leftovers from the creation of the world
He designed Richard III.
On the seventh day he took stock to see what else might be done.
The theatre directors had already covered the earth with posters,
And Shakespeare thought that after so much effort
He deserved to see a performance.
But first, as he was overtired,
He decided to die a little.

THE RUNNER

A deserted field,
Trodden down like a road,
And here and there
A book,

At great distances,
A basic book,
Firm as rock.

One is coming, panting with muscles,
Healthy as a new god,
And spits on it,
On each one in a row,
Steps on them heavenly.

He tires, he's had enough,
The field stretches ahead, deserted,
Trodden down like a road.
The runner collapses, dies,
Becomes a basic book, the last word,
A sign over which one cannot pass anymore.

Panting is heard,
From beyond a figure appears,
A runner stops, spits on the sign
And disappears over the horizon.

FRIENDS

Let's commit suicide, I said to my friends,
Today we've really understood each other,
We've been very depressed,
Never again will we reach
Such a peak of perfection
And it's a pity to waste the opportunity.

I think the bathroom's the most tragic place,
Let's do it like the enlightened Romans
Who opened their veins
While discussing the essence of love.
Look, I've warmed the water,
Let's make a start, dear friends, I'll count to three.

In hell I was somewhat surprised to find myself alone.
Perhaps some people don't die quite so easily
I told myself, or have ties.
I couldn't have made a mistake: making a pact's got to mean
                                                something.
But time went on. . .

I can assure you, it was quite hard for me in hell,
Especially at the start, as I was on my own,
There was no one there I could talk to,
But gradually I was accepted, made friends.

A very tightly knit group,
We discussed all sorts of theoretical questions,
We felt great,
We even got around to suicide.

And again, I found myself alone, in purgatory
Looking for a few kindred spirits,
Although the purgatorians were quite suspicious –
With their uncertain situation
Between two worlds –
A girl loves me, she's very beautiful.
We share moments of great ecstasy – unbelievable, fantastic!

And I feel almost like saying to her. . .
But having seen it all before, I let her do it first,
I wait and commit suicide afterwards,
Yet the girl somehow manages to come back to life —
And then I'm on my own in heaven —
No one's ever reached that far before,
I'm the first, the world exists only as a project,
Something very, very vague
In God's head,
I'm getting very friendly with him lately.

There's sadness at all levels,
Even God's desperate,
I look into his empty eyes and there lose myself.
He slips roaring down the precipice of my deaths,
We understand each other perfectly,
God, I think we've reached perfection,
You first,
How about leaving it all in the dark?

THE ILLNESS

I can feel something dying, Doctor,
It's here just around my being,
All my inside hurts,
During the day it's the sun that hurts,
And in the night it's the moon and stars.

I get a sharp pain in the cloud on the sky
Which I didn't even notice until today,
And I wake up every morning
With a sort of winter feeling.

I've taken all kinds of medicine, but it's done no good,
I've hated, and loved, I learned to read,
And I even read some books,
I talked to people and had a think,
I was good and I was handsome. . .

But none of it did any good, doctor,
And I've spent no end of years on it,

I think I must have caught death
One day
When I was born.

CHESS

I move a white day,
He moves a black day.
I advance with a dream,
He takes it to war.
He attacks my lungs,
I think for about a year in hospital.
I make a brilliant combination
And win a black day.
He moves a disaster
And threatens me with cancer
(Which moves for the moment in the shape of a cross)
But I put a book before him
He's obliged to retreat.
I win a few more pieces,
But, look, half my life
Is taken.
– If I give you check, you lose your optimism,
He tells me.
– It doesn't matter, I joke,
I'll do the castling of feelings.
Behind me my wife, children,
The sun, the moon and other onlookers
Tremble for every move I make.

I light a cigarette
And continue the game.

SYMMETRY

I was walking
When suddenly two roads opened
In front of me:
One to the right,
And one to the left,
Conforming to all rules of symmetry.

I stopped,
Screwed up my eyes,
Pursed my lips,
Coughed,
And set off on the one to the right
(Just the one I shouldn't have taken
As was later proved.)

I went on as best I could,
No need to give details.
And then in front of me opened two
Precipices:
One to the right,
One to the left.
I threw myself into the left,
Without even blinking, or jumping,
Just like a big heap into the one on the left,
Which, unfortunately, wasn't lined with feathers!
Crawling, I set off again.
I crawled for some time,
And suddenly in front of me
Two wide roads opened.
"I'll show you!" – I told myself,
And with grim determination,
I set off again on the one to the left.
Wrong, very wrong, the one on my right
Was the proper one, the real road, the great road.
And at the first crossroads
I gave myself totally
To the one on the right. Then the same again,
The other should have been the one, the other. . .

76

Now the food's almost gone,
My walking stick's aged,
Its buds no longer appear,
So I can rest in their shade.
When I become desperate.
Stones wear out my bones,
They creak and grumble at me
For one mistake after another. . .

And look, in front of me, opening again
Two skies:
One to the right,
One to the left.

*　*　*

I'm sorry for the butterflies
When I switch the light off,
And for the bats
When I switch it on. . .
Can't I move an inch
Without offending anyone?

So many strange things happen,
That I could always stay
Head in hands,
But an anchor thrown from heaven
Pulls them down. . .

The time isn't yet ripe
To rip the canvases,
Leave it.

Nichita Stănescu
(b. 1933 d. 1983)

A KIND OF QUIET IN BYBLOS

The diplomatic commuting has ended.
The whirlwind of burned smoke behind the plane
descends and speeds stunning
the dust on the sands.
Mothers in black, lie in wait at airports
watching through the curtain of rays.
The mutual exchange
of bodies of murdered soldiers
has begun.
Sacred scarabs roll again
in the desert,
earthly globes
the size of an adolescent's eye.
Millions of sacred scarabs, in the desert
roll millions of earthly globes
the size of an adolescent's eye.
Mothers in black lie in wait
at airports.
The mutual exchange of bodies
of murdered soldiers
has begun.
On beaches, on rocks, on sands,
are tanning the sacramental bodies
of adolescents,
their mothers, still dressed in white,
in red, in green and in violet,
lie in wait from a distance, sacramental and
with a hand to the mouth,
The dust from the sand shimmers
with red, iridescent gold.

SAD LOVE

Let's leave objectivity to the cog wheel,
to the bolt and the seal.
If time slips by the way it slips by me,
you don't have the right to watch me.

Let's leave to the happy ones the right
to drink water
because only they have mouths
and only they are thirsty.

But when I sleep, when I sleep
so deep
when I sleep the way I sleep
you surely don't have the right to get up
and leave.

THE LIGHTNING AND THE COLD

Dedicated to Nicolae Manolescu, literary critic

All of us in the courtyard, suddenly
uneasy, felt the presence of the wing.
It happened one Monday afternoon
a year ago.
For such a long time, especially in the evenings,
without saying a word to each other,
especially in the evenings, evening after evening,
we felt the uneasy presence of the wing
among ourselves in the courtyard.
Discretely we searched in the maple tree, in the barn, through the
sky-light,
or even under the big armchair in the dining room.
Also, we searched behind the family picture
in the rich frame, among the women's dresses in the wardrobe,
behind the velvet curtain, colored deep cherry.
Seemingly looking everywhere but there,
while talking about anything but that,
the presence of the wing was and still is unnerving us.
That's why the radio is always turned up,
and the noisy pump in the yard left to run.
Cats and dogs increased because of this,
and the bulb at the entrance
at night's left on.
Only recently, after a whole year,
while hurriedly leaving, called out by a patient,
I suddenly felt at my back
its cold breeze.
I stopped at the corner of the street
and turned my face like lightning to the house.
Ah, you, cold and lightning.
The angel is the very wall of the house,
the large wall, cut in the middle by a square window.
It's this very wall,
this one with the square window!
It's the very one
watching me, coldly.

AH, HOW MUCH WATER

Time becomes time
when it transforms into grass, into water,
into trees and into stones.
It is the only thing which has movement within it,
it is the only thing which passes
which ties and unties us
which becomes pregnant
by all that it meets on the way,
inventing its way,
giving birth to its way.
The only tangible thing is time,
objects are its movement.
Tigris and Euphrates,
ah, how much water!

FROM AN EVENING

I had to calm the dogs which had become restless
for no reason at all.
I had to ask for my glass to be changed
because suddenly I got a shock from it.
I had to look twice
to see if indeed it had passed by, very close to me,
near the lamplight from the garden,
that bird which proved that it had passed
and wasn't fluorescent green, as it had seemed to me,
but its usual grey.
That's why I'm writing this letter to you now
To ask you not to think about me anymore in the evenings
with such thoughts
and to assure you once more
that I haven't killed he whom I promised you
I'd leave alive.

Good bye.

SELF-PORTRAIT

I am nothing more than
a stain of blood
that speaks.

A CONFESSION

I can't yet raise an anthem to the stillness
for which I long and for which I hunger.
Not one house where I've stayed
kept me long inside it.
I long to be able to live
in my own words,
but clumsily through their doors
my body leans towards the animal kingdom.
Gladly I'd render to dogs that which is dogs
and to the maple trees that which is theirs,
but for me the howling of dogs is banned,
and the smell of maple trees forbidden.
I'd have to be able to rise much higher,
I'd have to throw away this ballast, –
but just the thought that what's above
might be exactly like that below, –
troubles me, so that I find
every throw has no direction
and static is every rejection.

UNTAMING

From too much black I'm white
from too much sun I'm night
from too much life more dead am I
only in dream myself am I
come to me from head to heel
to roll ourselves into a wheel
come to me, you, yet without you
so that I can be me, with me
O leaven, leaven, leaven
on my inferno be a heaven
O, stay, stay, stay
my palms nail and lay
on the cross of flesh
while the world rests.

SONG

The thinking body, now ugly, had evolved,
the words were said in an ancient and barbaric tongue.
To live had become 'I had lived' –
Inside me death had begun.

A patch of shadow crossed over me;
it was only from a vulture rising to fly
which was interrupting, gracefully,
the place where I was born,
from that where I shall die.

Sun, burning with cries, who keens for you
with his eyes?

SHE

Just now, just now
when I love her most,
just now I lied to her.
Just now, just now
when she's most fond of me,
just now I cast a shadow on her.
Just now, just now
when she's thinking about me
I'm singing my sorrows.
Just now, just now
when she's the most beautiful in the world
of my stars,
I go blind.
Just now, just now
when I feel her grace
penetrating all the walls of the town
I go deaf.
Just now, just now
when I feel that she is longing for me
I'm hurting my friends
unable to bear how much I long for her.
Just now, just now
when for my sake she irons
the gingham dress,
I stand and clean spears with petrol
To throw them at vultures and beasts.
Just now, just now
when I should be
filled with tender running,
I'm reaching for dreams
for fear of being happy.
Just now, just now
when she radiates light from her heart,
I read about the nova
and all the exploded stars
and I stretch like the longest street in town
and I pave
and dress in snow and ice,
especially ice,

especially ice, especially ice,
so that she, darling and divine
in passing, slips,
falls and hurts her ankle,
which, God,
I haven't kissed for such a long time.
After all,
who has the courage to kiss an ankle
if it isn't limping?!

WATCHING HER – MY MOTHER

On this loved one fell
all the time I have lived,
on this loved one shone
all my lived time.
I couldn't tear my glance away
from this loved one
I had eyes only to see her
my loved one.
I had arms only to embrace her
my loved one.
Suddenly, I saw my mother see her
this loved one.
On this loved one
time falls and snows.
Looking at my loved one
my mother cries.

MISTAKEN SKY

The vultures were flying upturned
and with claws turned upwards
to steal, as they would lambs,
the star with undulated light;

To steal, from above, as they would lambs,
the light of my eyes.

The vultures were flying upturned
and on their backs through the sky
their spines dropped
and rubbed against my breastbone.

Their sky was my body of flesh,
their earth the light of my eyes
from above.

HIEROGLYPHIC

What loneliness
not to understand the meaning
when there is a meaning

And what loneliness
to be blind in broad daylight, –
and deaf, what loneliness
when the song's in full swing

But not to understand
when there's nothing to understand
and to be blind in the middle of the night
and deaf when silence is absolute, –
Oh, loneliness of loneliness!

Ion Stoica
(b. 1936)

THE SPELL

Who e'er may do you harm
Let hemlock spring from his bed,
May the good stop his turn,
And night lie long in his head,
May all his days be mad
And draw luck that's bad
Like a hare draws cabbages to him,
May a stork's nest in winter hold him,
Let fire burn him!
And for you, good maiden,
Dreams of the moon with sleep are laden,
Above fields of tranquillity,
Autumns with a taste of honey
May dress you now in peaceful swathes,
May you have the stars for guards
Near your slumbers with the flowers
Awaiting you in the early hours
Herald of happy days above
The narrow beam of sun,
With news of love
From me will come

THE TRIAL

Do you confess that from time to time
You step out of line,
And profess
That the sighs of the world bore you?
– I confess!
– Do you deny that you set yourself high
Above others and on
Request would dare for the whole world
Acclaimed by it?
– I don't deny it!
– Do you admit that sometimes you dream night
After night, conquering yourself in flight
Believing
That in the gardens of heaven you can sit?
– This I admit!
– Do you recall in how many meadows
You forgot the commandments,
Stealing
Secret loves
Like an outlaw, too!
– I do!
– Does it happen in your forest you stand looking
In vain for oaks fearless of lopping
And winds of disgust burn under your brow?
– It does now.
– Don't you ever creep under the evenings
Full of mud and sighing under burdens,
Wondering
If your star was heavenless?
– Oh, yes!
– Isn't it true that in your humble mind
One day you found a knife
And still considering yourself pure and kind
You kept mute?
– It's the truth!
– Sometimes during long nights you search
But yourself you cannot reach
And you're afraid
And in your room the silence screams?

– That's how it seems.

*

The verdict is unanimous:
The greatest punishment applying:
An eternity of waiting
In an eternity of loneliness

I SHOULD HAVE LIKED. . .

I should have liked to cut the light
To make me a hood from that night
When the seeds of the world burst open
And began their eternal flight,
And to have been at midhour,
In its first innocence,
When under the eyes of day
Not one moment had begun
And to burn in four winds
By horizons of waiting,
Guilty of the beginning
Of each drop of sun,
And to have cried a sea,
To have bled in rivers,
And to have melted through time
In bewildered flowing,
To have felt pain
Petrifying into mountains
And the spring of dreams
In the garden of the first wedding,
And near the condemned shadow
To have changed the night
Heavy with hatred
Into a flowering leaf
And from mists of legend
In the flow of history
To see myself clearly in the water of the day
As in my mirror whose duty's
Not to wound me any more with
Cold light, waxen faces,
My moments able to look down,
My sky to have had a ladder

DECALOGUE

Thou shalt not take anything but dreams on thy way,
Put as many as you like in your treasure hold,
If the road is long and hard
They keep you from hunger, thirst and cold.
Thou shalt give only words as gifts
Their river does not freeze,
Among all your wealth,
For time's reckoning keep only these.
Thou shalt not stay in a lone star,
The highest is still falling,
Worlds are cut out from the lights
And from unfulfilled waiting.
Thou shalt not come from a forgotten night,
Go, together with the day through the copse,
It is a soul of the day where
All the moments of the world are pressed.
Thou shalt not listen to the voice of cold winters,
Fear of time slipping on the snow,
When the sand from the hours is burning you
Stay in the orchard under autumn's apple bough.
Thou shalt not fly all the summer in the flock,
Alone one evening cut across the field,
Without the terrors of night and wind
Joy has no price to yield.
Thou shalt not forget to look in mirrors,
In eyes, the book and the well,
From your face out of the depths, unknown
Thou shalt not run in the world afar;
Thou shalt not say that importance uplifts you
Deifying you in your noons,
Only the clouds make the peak forget
How near it is to the valley.
Thou shalt not swear on anything ever,
The gods are dying, lowered in the word.
The witness to all is only the distance
And cannot be reached by face and by wind;
Thou shalt not die before death
Keep the law which comes from the sky,
While the white light's within you
Thou shalt not die, not die, not die.

TRAPEZE

It's as if one's always
In a circus ring,
In a round valley walled by people,
On high, the trapeze,
In a noon of eyes,
Flying above hills of men,
Over walls alive with hope,
Holding their breath;
In your ears resound
The canons of the hearts beneath,
Because silence has leaden blood,
One aches with the uneasiness
Of those who call you to descend
And nothing seems easier
Than to give yourself to the void below

ORBIT

On the hour's threshold
Cry moments of yesterday
Lost from the fold,
Under the noise of the day
Valleys of silence
Vanish away;
On the threshold of love
A bitter tear
Is searching for home,
In a narrow gleam
The destiny of a star
Is stone;
A flight of words
Is heard passing
Through the sky much closer,
A face following
With eyes of air
And water;
Envious light
Is heard coming
From eternal watching,
In me is the night
When ways I wander
With pain;
Total unease in me
With a voice of steel
Calls me to be bridegroom
And all things are possible
And all things forbidden
Ad infinitum;
Towards seas of temptation
Which always soothe
The sad stream's glance,
I am held in orbit
By a heavy ball
Of chance.

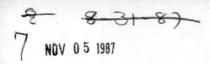